LIFE CYCLES

LIFE CYCLES

MICHAEL ELSOHN ROSS

ILLUSTRATED BY GUSTAV MOORE

THE MILLBROOK PRESS   BROOKFIELD, CONNECTICUT

To my friends Summer and Sunshine—M.R.

To Uncas Farms, where the cycles of nature
endlessly revolve.—G.M.

Library of Congress Cataloging-in-Publication Data
Ross Michael Elsohn, 1952–
Life cycles / by Michael Elsohn Ross ; illustrated by Gustav Moore.
p. cm.-(Cycles)
ISBN 0-7613-1817-8 (lib. bdg.)
1. Life cycles (Biology)—Juvenile literature. [1. Life cycles (Biology)
I. Moore, Gustav ill. II. Title
QH501 .R66 2001
571.8—dc21   00-056622

Published by The Millbrook Press, Inc.
2 Old New Milford Road
Brookfield, Connecticut 06804
www.millbrookpress.com

All plants and animals live and then die.
New plants and animals are born, and these grow and also die.
These patterns of life and death repeat over and over and over.
They are called life cycles.

SEED TO SUNFLOWER

One spring day Carrie plants a sunflower seed. This is the beginning of the sunflower's life cycle. The next week a small sprout pokes up, wearing its seed hull like a hat. When the hull falls off, two seed leaves spread out to bathe in the sunlight.

The little sunflower plant grows, and Carrie measures it. At first it only reaches her ankle, but by the Fourth of July it nudges her knees.

Two weeks later it tickles her tummy, and by August it is taller than she is.

Flower buds appear, and in a couple of more weeks it's taller than her dad. It grows and grows, and the buds soon open into big yellow flowers with rays like the sun. Bees buzz about and fertilize the flowers, causing seeds to form.

By the time Carrie goes back to school,
the sunflowers droop with the weight of seeds
and their withered petals fall to the ground.
In September chickadees hang upside down from the
flower head and pluck seeds. Carrie also collects the
seeds, and she stores them in an envelope.

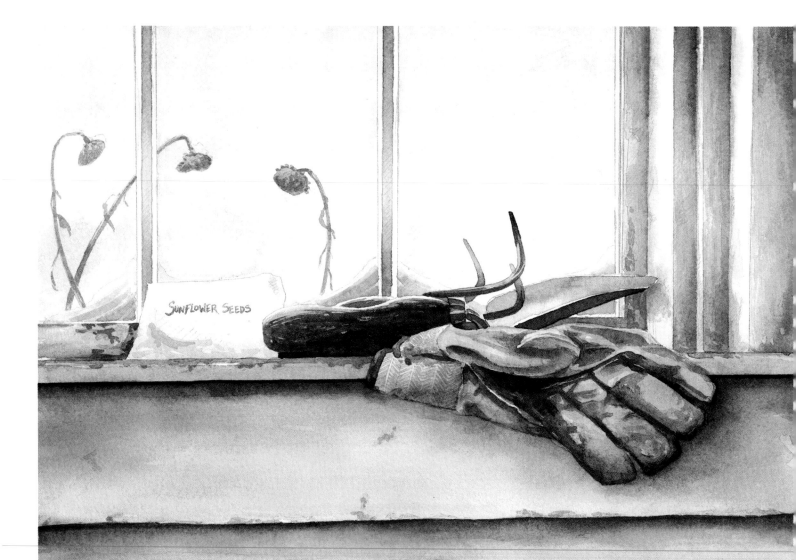

All winter and spring Carrie's seeds rest in the garden shed.
The old sunflower plant dies and then falls to the ground.
One spring day Carrie plants one of the seeds.
Soon it sprouts, and so begins another sunflower life cycle.

SUNFLOWER FACTS

- Sunflowers turn to face the sun as its position changes in the sky.
- Sunflowers are related to dandelions, lettuce, and daisies.
- The tallest sunflowers are over ten feet high.

MUSHROOM JOURNEY

Deep in the forest, a mushroom stands among
the moss and old twigs.

It is part of a fungus that feeds underground
on dead plants and animals. The mushroom has a cap
that looks like an umbrella. Under it are gills covered
with thousands of tiny spores.

Each day spores fall and ride far away on the forest breezes.
They land in many places where they cannot grow.
One lands on a fox's nose, another settles on a rock,
and another crashes into a puddle.
But one little spore ends up on some moist dead leaves,
which is just the right kind of place to grow.

MAGNIFIED SPORES

This is the beginning of the mushroom's life cycle.
The little spore sends out a tube that divides into threads.
Nearby is another spore from the same kind of mushroom.
When their threads touch they begin to grow together
into a new fungus. Each day it grows bigger and bigger,
until it is big enough to make a mushroom.

At first the mushroom looks like a button, but as
the stalk grows, the button becomes a cap.
The cap opens, showing gills covered with tiny spores.
Each day the spores fall from the gills
and ride in the forest breeze.

Many land in places where they cannot grow,
but one lands on some moist dead leaves
where it sends out a tiny tube.
So begins another mushroom life cycle.

MUSHROOM FACTS

- There are thousands of different kinds of mushrooms.
- Some wild mushrooms are poisonous.
- Certain mushrooms grow as big as a person's head, while others are as small as a raisin.

FROM EGG TO EGG

One warm May afternoon, a little head pokes out from a tiny egg hidden in the ground. It's a baby grasshopper beginning its life cycle. Though she is smaller than a sunflower seed, she is as hungry as a lion. With her sharp jaws she munches leaves and grows.

She grows so much that soon she must crawl out of her old skin and then wait for her new, bigger skin to harden. Each day she munches more and more leaves. Each day she grows.

As summer passes she sheds her skin two more times.
Now she has little wing pads on her back and large hind legs
that help her jump far away from hungry predators.

By the end of July she sheds her skin once more.
Now she has wings and a long egg-laying tube.
In the shadows of the grasses she meets a male grasshopper.
He plays music to her by scraping his leg against his wing,
and she moves closer to mate.

Later she lays her eggs and leaves them behind in the soft soil. In October the cold comes, and many plants lose their leaves. The grasshopper has no food and soon dies, but her eggs are protected in the ground. All winter they lie hidden under leaves and snow.

One May day a little head pokes out from a tiny egg. It's a baby grasshopper and the beginning of another grasshopper life cycle.

GRASSHOPPER FACTS

- Grasshoppers lay eggs in pods with 20-150 eggs.
- Some grasshoppers can jump up to 20 times the length of their bodies. That would be like a person jumping over a 12-story building.
- Adult grasshoppers have four wings and six legs.

All living things—whether a person, a sunflower, a mushroom, or a grasshopper—have a life cycle. The life cycle of a grasshopper might take just a few months to complete, while the life cycle of a person can take many years.

ABOUT THE AUTHOR AND ARTIST

Michael Elsohn Ross lives at the entrance of Yosemite National Park, California, on a bluff overlooking the wild Merced river. Both his wife and teenage son are published poets and avid outdoors people. For more than twenty-five years Michael has been teaching visitors to Yosemite about the plants, animals, and geology of the park. He leads classes and backpack trips for the Yosemite Association and is the educational director of Yosemite Guides. His work in the park and as a science educator have inspired him to write more than thirty books for young people, including **Become a Bird and Fly** and **Earth Cycles**, the first volume in the Cycles series.

Growing up in rural Maine, Gustav Moore's boyhood adventures in the woods and fields of his family's farm have given him a deep appreciation and love of the natural world. His colorful and detailed watercolor paintings reflect the beauty and wonder of nature. He has illustrated three books for children: **Stonewall Secrets**, which was recognized as a 1998 Notable Children's Book by **Smithsonian** magazine, **Everybody's Somebody's Lunch**, and **Earth Cycles**. Gustav Moore works and lives in Maine, where he still wanders the open pastures of the family farm, finding inspiration in the cycles of nature.